CONVERSATIONS
ON PURPOSE

With love,

Mary
Stahl

CONVERSATIONS ON PURPOSE

This book will encourage conversation between all age groups and all generations. All 100 questions are safe, fun, and are guaranteed to connect you with others.

MARY STAHL

ISBN: 1530686792
ISBN 13: 9781530686797

"True happiness arises in the first place,
from the enjoyment of one's self, and in the
next, from the friendship and conversation
of a few select companions."

– Joseph Addison

ACKNOWLEDGEMENTS

I AM THANKFUL FOR PARENTS who always showed up – to everything! Without them I have no doubt I would not be who I am today. My mom still comes to church every Sunday and sits by me on the front row. (My husband is the Pastor) and I know my dad, who is not living today would say, "Great book! When's the next one going to be finished?" I am grateful.

I am thankful for my husband, Dr. Daniel R. Stahl. While he is more accomplished than I am and more talented in other areas than I am, he is a continual encouragement to me in fulfilling my purpose and passions. He champions my dreams, he covers me in prayer, and he proofreads everything! He helps, he serves, he challenges, he pushes, he loves, he gives, he answers all my questions, and he promotes us. I am grateful.

Being a Pastor's wife is hard especially when it comes to thanking specific people because of the fear of leaving someone out. I have to say that all my girlfriends, especially my Life Group and the people at The Palms Church have been huge encouragers to me. I am thankful for their faith and love for me. Their transparent and brave stories inspire me. I love all my friends who have pushed me to grow and move out and "Do It!" I am grateful!

I am grateful for you, the READER! Purchasing this book means that you are on a quest for more: You want to know more, love more, and connect more! That is awesome. Without an audience there would not be a purpose or impact. I am grateful for you!

I give a special thank you to to Ed and Christi Vila and Gail Johnson for your continual love and support to me during the publication and writing of this book. I am grateful for you.

DEDICATION

I dedicate this book to my son Benjamin Mark Greer. He was born on May 11, 1999, with a congenital heart defect and Down's syndrome. At 32 days old he survived an incredible heart surgery that rebuilt his heart. With the help of lots of therapy, Benjamin first learned sign language, then tongue movement, and finally voice and word formation. He speaks today with volume and increased pronunciations. Our conversations continue and grow the more we talk, read, and sing. On Thursday nights around the table he begins, "Today is thankful Thursday Mom, what you happy for."

May you never stop talking and gaining insights with the people that truly matter.

Communicate on Purpose - Change the World

BENJAMIN

THINK ABOUT IT?

EMPTY NESTERS: OUR KIDS ARE grown and we need new and fresh topics to talk about when we are together, out on the town, or sitting around the table.

 YES   NO

I AM NETWORKING with a new group of people and I would love conversation starters that would help unite and connect our group.

 YES   NO

I NEED TO CONNECT with a different generation whether it be our kids at dinner or my parents when we are out - questions that will fill the silence and lead to great conversation.

 YES   NO

I NEED TOPICS to talk about on a date night with my spouse besides: babies, schedule, money, or other people. I want happy conversation about US!

 YES   NO

If you answered "YES" to any of these questions, then welcome to your new favorite book.

Congratulations: Just one question can lead to a myriad of insights about people you may not know or people you have known for decades.

How to use
this book

Take it on dates with kids or with your spouse. My husband and I keep one in each car. We take it into restaurants when we go out and take it to family gatherings. Our kids moan when we pull out "the book", but we usually end up staying way longer than expected and laughing a whole lot more. Once on a date night, the waiter asked us if we were newlyweds because we were talking and engaged with each other so much more compared to everyone else.

Take it with you when you go out with other people. My husband usually sets up the conversation with, "Hey, Mary has this book that she brings out on our dates. It is a question book and we love it." He thought it was kinda dorky at first, but not now. "Honey, do you have it in your purse?" he asks. True story. We rarely go out without our book.

BY ALL MEANS TAKE YOUR book to EVERY extended family holiday, vacation, or gathering. You will discover more about the people you think you know, than you can imagine. Use it just sitting around the beach, the table, the waiting room, the turkey, the mall, the kids, the park, or on a road trip.

HAVE THIS BOOK AROUND THE DINNER TABLE at meal time (we keep one in the kitchen drawer). Let different family members pick a question. Allow pause time for people to think and then let each person share their answer. You will be amazed how reluctant talkers will open and respond to structured questions. *Conversations On Purpose* will ignite relationships!

1.

What vacation would you want to do all over again? What made that time together so memorable?

2.

Talk about your first
memory as a child.
How old were you?

3.

If you had a family treasure chest what three favorite memories would you put into the treasure chest?

4.

What is your favorite home-cooked meal? Are there specific memories associated with eating that meal?

❖ ❖ ❖

5.

When you have been sick, what were some of the kindest things one of your family members or friends did for you?

❖ ❖ ❖

6.

What is a great gift someone has given you?

7.

Talk about your ancestors and where they came from. How far back can you trace your family tree?

8.

If you had to describe yourself to a person moving into your home for an extended stay, would you describe yourself as a morning person or a late night person? What would they need to know about you so they could keep you happy.

❖ ❖ ❖

9.

What game do you like to play with others? When was the last time you played that game?

❖ ❖ ❖

10.

Are you a person who needs quiet time to re-charge or does being around other people recharge you?

11.

A tradition does not have to revolve around a holiday. Growing up what were some family events that became traditions?

12.

Have you ever been pulled over by a cop? What was the story behind you being pulled over?

13.

What is one thing about your house that you would change tomorrow if you could?

14.

Everyone goes through tough times. What is something you have learned that has helped you get through a tough time?

15.

Talk about a Christmas present that was very meaningful or special to you. Who gave it to you and how old were you?

16.

Who was your best friend growing up? What did you like most about that friend?

17.

There is a common saying that states, "A friend sticks closer than a brother." Talk about a time when someone stuck close to your side through a situation when no one else showed up.

❖ ❖ ❖

18.

What is one quality about each person in the room that you particularly appreciate about them?

19.

What is something your friends or family members do for you that you probably take for granted? In other words, if they stopped doing this, you would REALLY miss this act of kindness.

20.

What is your favorite room in your house? What makes that space wonderful?

21.

Did you play outside as a child? What were your favorite outdoor activities?

22.

What activity or hobby do you enjoy watching others do?

23.

Talk about a pet that you liked the most. Which family member took care of that pet and where did the pet sleep at night?

24.

Growing up, how did you get to school?

25.

Do you like your bedroom? Pretend you could redesign it. What would you keep and what would you change?

26.

Nobody is perfect. If you could stop one bad habit or change one thing about your-self what would it be and how do you think that would affect you?

27.

What is your favorite holiday and season of the year and what do you love most about that time?

28.

Have you ever been in a scary situation? How did you get through that time?

29.

Growing up did your mom or dad read you stories or sing you songs? What books and songs did you enjoy?

30.

If your family was moving into a very small house boat for one year, what are five items, which are not electronic, that you would take with you? (not living essentials like food, clothing, or money.)

❖ ❖ ❖

31.

If we lived in a culture where style and a person's personal appearance DID NOT MATTER AT ALL, what would you wear and how would your grooming change?

32.

What is your full name?
How did you get it?
Where does it come
from?

33.

What is one quality about yourself that you like? How does that characteristic enhance your everyday life?

34.

Growing up as a child, what was one of your favorite shows to watch on television?

35.

When you are on vacation, are you a beach person, a mountain person, a big city person, or a stay at home and chill type of person?

36.

What was a family tradition you used to do as a kid on either Easter or Christmas?

37.

Many people dress up and wear costumes for Halloween or costume parties. Talk about one of the memorable costumes you have dressed up in.

❖ ❖ ❖

38.

Have you ever spent time reading the Bible and what do you remember about it?

39.

What is a movie you have seen more than one time and you would watch again this week if you had the time? What about that movie compels you to watch it more than once?

40.

Who is your favorite musician or genre of music?

41.

Are you a listener
of: talk radio, music,
sports, or audio books?
What do you most like
about them?

❖ ❖ ❖

42.

What was the first car you ever owned? Tell the story behind how you got it.

43.

Would you prefer going to a live musical, an opera, a Broadway play, or poetry reading?

❖ ❖ ❖

44.

What New Year's resolution or other goals have you made that you actually accomplished?

45.

What was one of the greatest things you have ever done for yourself? People may have not agreed with you; but, you did it and it was good for you.

46.

If you could take a class to learn more about something, what class would you take and why?

47.

People spend hours of their time watching television, video, and on social media. If television and social media did not exist, what would you do with your time?

48.

What is something that you really enjoy that you have not done in a while? When is the next time you might be able to enjoy this activity?

49.

What favorite subject did you enjoy in school and what did you enjoy most about it?

50.

Have you ever had a personal mentor or someone in life that really impacted you? How did they influence you and what was their main message that inspired you?

51.

Let's talk about smiling.
Are you a person who
smiles a lot? Come up
with seven benefits that
happen when someone
smiles.

52.

Can you recall a time when someone gave you money without expecting anything in return? Recall what happened and how that made you feel.

53.

What is something about you that no one in this conversation knows about you?

54.

What foods do you generally feel like eating when you are stressed or needing comfort?

55.

They say the average person has five jobs or career changes over their lifetime. What career change would you want next if you knew it would provide financially?

56.

Do you have a routine or a ritual that you do every day that has helped make life better or more productive? Share your success tips.

57.

When you are with friends do you tend to be the listener or the talker?

58.

When you are sick or in the hospital do you like people to visit you, bring meals, stay close, or do you prefer to be by yourself?

59.

Would you prefer lunch at a friend's house or a meal with your friend at a restaurant?

60.

If you and a friend could do something that you have NEVER done before, what would it be? What friend would you bring along?

61.

If your friends had to complete a mission together, what role would you be most comfortable filling? Leader, planning/co-ordinator, treasurer, or just along for the ride.

❖ ❖ ❖

62.

Go around the room with your friends and name one quality about each friend that you hope never changes.

63.

Growing up who was your best friend and what kind of things did you do together? Do you still keep in touch?

64.

Have you been on an overnight trip with your friends? Talk about that trip and who was with you?

65.

Talk about gifts that your friends have gotten you in the past for a special occasion? What were they and what made them so special?

66.

When going on an out-ing with a friend, do you prefer to drive or ride along? Do you like the radio on or off?

67.

What type of person were you when you were younger? After everyone has shared, determine who you think you would have hung out with.

68.

It has been said that a true friend walks in the door when everyone else walks out. Talk about a time in your life when one of your friends supported you in a tough time.

69.

What is one of the biggest dreams or tasks that you've yet to accomplish? What do you need to do in order to finish?

70.

What sports or school activities were you involved in when you were younger?

71.

Were you an outgoing student or a shy student? Did you enjoy sports, music, dance, or books?

72.

What is one thing you used to do when you were younger that you still do as an adult?

73.

Have you ever sung Karaoke? If so, what is your "go to" karaoke song?

If you are not a karaoke singer, and all your friends would sing with you? What would be your "go to" karaoke song?

❖ ❖ ❖

74.

What is an outing you would like to do if someone planned it?

75.

Are you a book reader
or a movie watcher?

76.

Describe your child-
hood bedroom.

77.

If you could reinvent yourself what qualities would you add into your life?

78.

If you have children, what has been the biggest struggle about being a parent?

79.

Speaking from a child's perspective: What has been the biggest struggle in getting along with your parents and what has been the greatest strength or joy about knowing your parents?

❖ ❖ ❖

80.

Did you have a club house or hide out growing up? Where do you go now when you want to be alone?

81.

If you had a group of friends that you could spend the day hanging out with, what would you enjoy doing?

82.

Share vacation ideas: What has been the most memorable vacation you have taken with your family that your friends might be able to do with their families?

83.

How has busyness or
lack of time influenced
your relationships?

❖ ❖ ❖

84.

Have you ever been to a different country? What was one of the highlights?

85.

Who encourages you and helps you feel great about life? What do they do to encourage you?

❖ ❖ ❖

86.

If you could change your name what would you change it to?

87.

If you could be a superhero for a year, who would you be and why?

88.

What was the first musical record, CD, or download you ever purchased?

89.

If you could be good
at a new hobby, what
would it be?

90.

When traveling with
a friend, do you get
separate hotel rooms
or stay in the same
room? Why would you
make that decision?

91.

If you had to get rid of one electronic device forever which one would it be?

92.

Have you ever been to a wedding other than your own? What do you love or not like about weddings?

93.

Have you ever been on a cruise? Where did you go and what about your trip did you love?

❖ ❖ ❖

94.

What charity work have you been involved in? What was your role and what did you do?

95.

What is one thing that you used to do that you are glad you do not do anymore?

96.

What do you recall most about some of the prettiest places you have ever visited?

97.

Do you watch YOU TUBE videos? Who are some of your favorite YOU TUBERS?

98.

Talk about a life-lesson you've learned and who or what might have helped you understand it.

99.

Talk about the greatest movies or books you have seen or read.

❖ ❖ ❖

100.

What is your favorite dessert?

Bonus Section: Would you rather

Would you rather fly in a four seater plane at night and reach your destination in 2.5 hours or travel by bus during the day and reach your destination in 20 hours?

Would you rather give up brushing your teeth for a year or give up indoor plumbing for a year?

Would you rather be outside and caught in a thunder and lightning storm or outside in a blizzard?

Would you rather walk down a crowded beach without clothes on or walk through the deep dark jungle with a guide?

Would you rather lose your eyesight or lose your ability to walk?

Would you rather walk across hot fiery coals or jump through a hole that has been cut through the ice and into the water below?

Would you rather have quadruplets or a child every year for four years?

Would you rather have bad breath or bad body odor?

Would you rather walk through a field of sleeping alligators or paddle board through water with sharks?

Would you rather eat a jar of hot peppers or eat a can of anchovies?

Would you rather give up your cell phone or give up your pet?

Would you rather be stuck in a room with ten large snakes or hundreds of spiders?

Would you rather be on a technology free bus full of toddlers and young children or on a bus full of 12 and 13 year olds?

Would you rather want to be poor and happy or rich and sad?

Would you rather want to be the most popular person in school or have two really great friends?

Would you rather do all your shopping online or all your shopping at stores?

Would you rather live without running water or without electricity?

Would you rather give up toilet paper or give up eating utensils?

ABOUT THE AUTHOR

 MARY WAS RAISED IN CENTRAL Florida and graduated from South-eastern University in Lakeland, Fla. She is a retired junior high school teacher and a Certified Life Coach. She now dedicates her time to raising her teenage son, training and mentoring leaders, as well as developing and teaching work-shops that help people reach their full potential. She also spends her time helping her husband at the church, traveling, and speaking at conferences and meetings with the purpose of inspiring people to find and live with purpose and hope. One unique thing about Mary is that she has an identical twin sister named Helen. They live 15 minutes from each other and they both care for their aging mother who has Dementia.

For more information on Mary and her speaking schedule, bookings, the online store, or to submit a question for her next book, you may visit

http://www.marystahl.tv